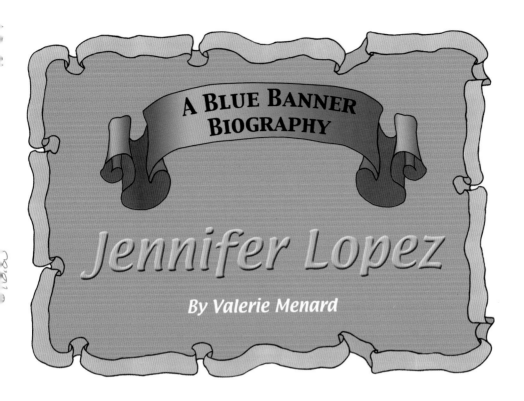

A BLUE BANNER BIOGRAPHY

Jennifer Lopez

By Valerie Menard

Claymont Schools
Intermediate L.R.C.

Mitchell Lane
PUBLISHERS

P.O. Box 196
Hockessin, Delaware 19707
Visit us on the web: www.mitchelllane.com
Comments? email us: mitchelllane@mitchelllane.com

Printing   2   3   4   5   6   7   8   9

Blue Banner Biographies

Eminem	Sally Field	Jodie Foster
Melissa Gilbert	Rudy Giuliani	Ron Howard
Michael Jackson	**Jennifer Lopez**	Nelly
Mary-Kate and Ashley Olsen	Daniel Radcliffe	Selena
Shirley Temple	Richie Valens	Rita Williams-Garcia
Jay Z	Ja Rule	Missy Elliott
Bow Wow		

Library of Congress Cataloging-in-Publication Data
Menard, Valerie.
    Jennifer Lopez/Valerie Menard.
        p. cm. — (A blue banner biography)
    Includes index.
    Summary: Looks at the life and career of "J. Lo," who decided at an early age to become an entertainer and is reputed to be the highest-paid Latina actress in Hollywood history, as well as being a successful singer and dancer.
    Filmography: p.
    ISBN 1-58415-225-7 (Library Bound)
    1. Lopez, Jennifer, 1970—Juvenile literature. 2. Actors—United States—Biography—Juvenile literature. 2. Actors—United States—Biography—Juvenile literature. 3. Singers—United States—Biography—Juvenile literature. [1. Lopez, Jennifer, 1970- 2. Actors and actresses. 3. Singers. 4. Women—Biography. 5. Hispanic Americans—Biography.] I. Title. II. Series.
    PN2287.L634M46 2003
    791.43′028′092—dc21
                                                                                2003008857

ABOUT THE AUTHOR: Valerie Menard is a freelance writer. She was hired as an editor for *Hispanic* magazine when the magazine moved from Washington, D.C. to Austin, Texas in July 1994 and remained with the magazine through 1999, when it relocated to Miami, Florida. Before joining the magazine she was the managing editor for five years of an Austin bilingual weekly, *La Prensa.* At *La Prensa,* Valerie became an expert on the Hispanic market and an advocate for Latino causes. At *Hispanic,* she promoted stories that addressed the important political and social issues facing Latinos. As a freelance writer she has written for several publications including: *The Austin American Statesman, Estylo, Latina Style, Red Herring, Hispanic,* and *Vista.* She has also written biographical books for children as part of the *Real-Life Reader Biography* series and in 2000, her first solo book project, *The Latino Holiday Book,* was published by Marlowe and Company. The book is in its fifth printing and the Spanish version was published in 2002 by Random House Español.

PHOTO CREDITS: Cover: AP Photo; p. 4 Getty Images; p. 6 Globe Photos; p. 9 Globe Photos; p. 13 Shooting Star; p. 15 AP Photo; p. 18 AP Photo; p. 20 AP Photo; p. 23 Getty Images; p. 24 AP Photo; p. 28 Getty Images

CONTENTS

Jennifer has always wanted to succeed in more than one arena. Today she is a successful actress and recording artist.

Girl from the Bronx

*L*atinos captured a lot of headlines toward the end of the twentieth century, and one of the most prominent young Latinos of the nineties and the new millenium was Jennifer Lopez. From the time she won her first major movie role in *Mi Familia* in 1995 to when she released her third successful record, *This is Me...Then*, in 2002, Jennifer has taken full advantage of every opportunity that has come her way. In 2003, she was reportedly the highest paid Latina actress in Hollywood history. Her determination will help her continue to grow as one of America's biggest stars.

Jennifer knew early on that she not only wanted to be a star but that she didn't want to succeed in just one arena, like movies or music. She wanted to be like her idols who were successful in films and had top-selling records. "I want everything," she told a reporter

Jennifer comes from a musical family. She's shown here performing on NBC's Today Show *Summer Concert Series in 2001.*

for *Entertainment Weekly.* "I want family. I want to do good work. I want love. I want to be comfortable. I think of people like Cher and Bette Midler and Diana Ross and Barbara Streisand. That's always been the kind of career I've hoped to have. I want it all."

Her attraction to the entertainment industry was not unusual. For Jennifer, it was in her genes. Her mother, Guadalupe, and her sisters, Lynda and Leslie (Jennifer is the middle sister), all have musical abilities. Lynda is a disc jockey in New York and Leslie is a music teacher. "This is a musical family," wrote Martha Frankel in an article for *In Style* magazine. "All four women have wonderful, rich voices."

Jennifer is a native of New York City, born in the Bronx on July 24, 1970. Jennifer says she knew by the age of five, when she began to take dancing lessons, that she wanted to be an entertainer. She attended Holy Family School, a Catholic private school, where she studied dance, theater, and music, as well as regular classes.

She enjoyed acting and would pretend to be her favorite television characters for fun. One of the most popular shows in the seventies was *Charlie's Angels*. It was about three beautiful former policewomen, played by Kate Jackson, Farrah Fawcett, and Jaclyn Smith, who were hired by a rich man to work as private detectives. Jennifer, Leslie, and Lynda would act out the show, with each girl taking the part of her favorite character. Because of her light hair, Jennifer would play Farrah Fawcett's character, Jill.

> *Jennifer says she knew by the age of five, when she began taking dancing lessons, that she wanted to be an entertainer.*

Many children dream of fame, but reaching that goal can take years, sometimes even a lifetime. Jennifer showed that she was unique at a young age. By the time she turned sixteen, she had already acquired acting experience in small parts and television commercials.

Her parents still hoped that she would give up acting and go to college to study law, but Jennifer had caught the acting bug and was not going to give up her dream. By the time she graduated from high school, she had decided to pursue her career as an entertainer. Her parents were upset at first—so much so that Jennifer left home and lived in a dance studio before getting an apartment with friends. Eventually, she was hired as a dancer to perform in a European tour of the show *Golden Miracles of Broadway.*

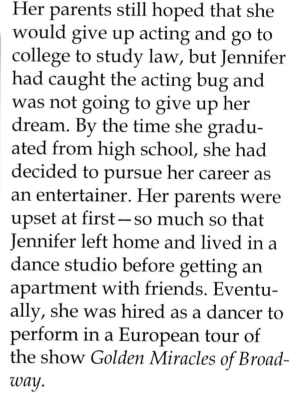

By the time Jennifer turned sixteen, she already had experience in television commercials.

Her parents always encouraged their children to be the best they could be. Her mother, Guadalupe, was born in Puerto Rico but raised in New York. Her father, David, was born in the U.S. but is also of Puerto Rican descent. Today, her mother is a kindergarten teacher and her father is an insurance company computer specialist. Jennifer grew up in a middle class family, in the Bronx, a section of New York City that has a

Jennifer (bottom right) as a part of the Fly Girls dance troupe from the Fox television show In Living Color.

large Latino population. "It wasn't so much a bad neighborhood as one where you had to be careful," she remembers. "I have a lot of street smarts because of the neighborhood I grew up in."

Her first big break in show business came in 1990 when she was only twenty. Jennifer auditioned for and was cast in the Fox television show *In Living Color*. Like *The Simpsons*, *In Living Color* was one of the first hit television shows for the new network. It launched the careers of many comedic actors, including the show's creator, Keenan Wayans, his brothers, and Jim Carrey. Jennifer was part of the show's dance troupe, known as the Fly Girls. They would dance at the show's opening, middle, and end. Jennifer beat out 2,000 girls who also auditioned.

Jennifer was cast in the movie Mi Familia by director Gregory Nava.

Five years later, Jennifer scored her first breakthrough into movies when she was cast in the movie *Mi Familia* by director Gregory Nava. Though she had had a small role in the 1986 film *My Little Girl*, this was a much bigger part. Although not a starring role, she impressed director Francis Ford Coppola, who cast her in his film *Blood and Wine.* Her co-star in that movie was Jack Nicholson. She also won a role in the movie *Money Train,* with Woody Harrelson and Wesley Snipes. But *Mi Familia,* which told the story of a Mexican American family through several generations, proved the most important because she got to work with director Nava. That association would help her earn yet another breakthrough two years later, when she was cast in the starring role in the movie *Selena.*

Selena

Selena Quintanilla Perez was only 23 years old when she died, but she had already touched the Latino community so deeply that she would never be forgotten. The Mexican-American native of Texas began singing Tejano tunes when she was a child. Her talent and charisma were so great that she achieved success extremely early. But her life ended on March 31, 1995, when she was murdered by the president of her fan club.

Latinos, especially in Texas, were devastated by the loss of Selena. News coverage of the event revealed that she had fans all over the country. Soon, people unfamiliar with her began to ask, "Who was Selena?" The story of Selena's life immediately caught the attention of Hollywood. It was time for the country to find out who she was. Selena's family asked director Gregory Nava to direct the film, and once he agreed, the next question was, "Who would play Selena?"

The chance to play Selena in a biopic (a movie about a real person's life) was a huge opportunity, especially for a Latina actress. Very few leading roles were offered to Latinos. Nava and Selena's father, Abraham Quintanilla, knew how important it was and how important this movie would be to the Latino community. They began a nationwide search for the actress who would play Selena. In cities like San Antonio, Los Angeles, and Chicago, Nava and his team issued open casting calls (when anyone, not just people with acting experience, can show up and audition for a part). It was through this process that Nava found the actress who would play Selena as a child, Becky Lee Meza. But finding the right girl to play Selena as a young woman was a bit more difficult, and it was getting political. The Latino community began to demand that the actress be Mexican-American, as Selena was. But in the end, Nava chose the actress with whom he had worked previously and who had some real film experience—Jennifer Lopez.

The role of Selena was the chance of a lifetime for Jennifer.

This was the kind of role about which any actress dreams. The story of Selena's life was triumphant as well as tragic. Jennifer was going to have to relate these

Jennifer performs in Selena

aspects of her life as well as stay true to Selena's image. As a star, Selena was friendly, generous, and very humble. Jennifer was going to have to express these same characteristics. How well she accomplished these challenges could determine her future success as an actress. As an early incentive, Jennifer acquired something that was also a first for Latino actors—money. She became the first Latina to receive $1 million for a movie role.

Jennifer became the first Latina to receive $1 million for a movie role when she accepted the part of Selena.

The budget for *Selena* was $18 million, the most any Latino film had received until then. The budget allowed for actresses like Jennifer and actors like Edward James Olmos, who played Abraham Quintanilla, and Jon Seda, who played Selena's husband, Chris Perez. But the pressure was on to make sure that the movie made money. But would audiences accept Jennifer as Selena? Jennifer also knew what was at stake. "This movie is the celebration of the life of an amazing person. Selena was someone who had not just tremendous talent but also a beautiful heart, and I think that's what her fans loved most about her," said Jennifer in *Hispanic* magazine. "I knew her memory was still fresh in their minds, so the most important thing for me was to get it right."

Jennifer wanted to capture Selena's personality down to the tiniest details.

Jennifer has earned a reputation for her hard work. Director Oliver Stone complimented her work in his film *U-Turn*, saying, "She's there at seven in the morning, ready to rehearse, knows all her lines, and is fearless about doing her own stunts." Jennifer used this work ethic when preparing for the role as Selena. She took special care to recreate Selena in every way. Once she was chosen for the part, she moved in with the Quintanillas and studied several family videos and home movies. "I didn't want to merely impersonate or caricature her," Jennifer told *Time* magazine. "I wanted to capture her personality, down to the tiniest details—even the way she rubbed her nose."

Her hard work paid off. When *Selena* opened in May 1997, it earned the biggest opening day revenue for a Latino film, about $12 million. It surpassed even the studio's expectations. Jennifer also received high praise for her performance, and Latinos clearly found her performance as Selena convincing. The moment was powerful as well for the young actress. Remembering her first reaction to the film when she saw it herself, Jennifer told Jeffrey Ressner of *Time,* "I wanted to play her as the vibrant, alive person she was, instead of as a victim. I never broke down—until I saw the finished film. Then it just ripped me apart, and I sobbed nonstop for 40 minutes."

> **When *Selena* opened in 1997, it earned the biggest opening day revenue for a Latino film up to that point.**

Many more movie roles for Jennifer would follow *Selena.* She co-starred in the thriller *Anaconda,* and in *Out of Sight.* She was also the voice of Azteca in the animated film *Antz.* But after *Selena,* her personal life would make its own U-turn and give Jennifer some valuable lessons.

Jennifer in Love

Jennifer Lopez seems fearless when it comes to how she lives her life. She's aggressive about her career, but also about love. Like many people who become famous, Jennifer's private life has become exposed to the public. Newspapers, television shows, and tabloids make many millions of dollars reporting on the lives of celebrities. Once *Selena* premiered, Jennifer would never again know privacy. But at the time, she was more concerned about planning her wedding.

Her choices in love have been wildly opposite, from a high school sweetheart to a hip-hop star with a police record. In some of the earliest interviews with Jennifer, she seemed completely devoted to her boyfriend at the time, David Cruz. They both went to the same high school. In a spring 1996 article in *Moderna* magazine, Christine Granados wrote, "The fast-paced

Jennifer with her then-boyfriend Sean "P. Diddy" Combs. The two eventually went their separate ways after their relationship was heavily publicized by the media.

life of Hollywood hasn't changed this *muchacha*. You won't see her party-hopping with the likes of Keanu Reeves or Brad Pitt. She is completely devoted to her high-school sweetheart, David Cruz. The precious little time she has away from work is saved for Cruz and her family."

But loving someone who has dreams of becoming a star isn't easy. For the partner of a celebrity, especially when that celebrity's career starts to take off, the shock may be too great. The days of leaving home unnoticed are over. Photographers will follow a celebrity anywhere, from the grocery store to a movie premiere. That's what seemed to happen to Jennifer and Cruz.

But by the time she won the lead role in *Selena*, Jennifer had already met the man she planned to marry. Jennifer first saw Ojani Noa at a restaurant owned by singer Gloria Estefan, Laros on the Beach, where he was waiting tables. For Jennifer, it was love at first sight. She supposedly told a friend, "That's the man I'm going to marry." They did start dating, and about a year later, on February 22, 1997, they were married. The marriage seemed sudden to many outsiders. Jennifer had just finished her role as Selena Quintanilla Pérez and was about to begin work on two new films, *Anaconda* and *U-Turn*. But according to an article in *In Style*, Jennifer seemed very much in love on her wedding day.

> **When Jennifer saw Ojani Noa at a restaurant, it was love at first sight.**

However, the pressures of Hollywood would hurt this marriage. As Jennifer began to win bigger and big-

After breaking up with rapper P. Diddy, Jennifer married choreographer Cris Judd in 2001. This marriage did not last long, either, and in 2002, the couple divorced.

ger roles in more popular films, the strain became obvious. They divorced within a year. She told *People*, "It's tough for me because the men I'm attracted to, for some reason, haven't gotten it together." Noa told the *New York Post*, "She wanted her career, so everything with us went out the window."

It wasn't long before she met her next love, rap star Sean "P. Diddy" Combs. At first, many people thought that this choice in men was another impetuous decision on her part. Jennifer revealed some of her compulsive nature when it comes to love in an article for *Vanity Fair*: "I'm an idiot when I fall in love. When I fall in love, everything else falls out the window." But she and Combs actually had more in common than many people thought. They both grew up in the tougher parts of New York, they're both former dancers and entertainers (Combs is a successful hip-hop artist like Jennifer), and they're both very aggressive when it comes to success. Before getting his big break as a rapper, Combs was an intern for a record company.

In November 2002, Jennifer announced plans to marry movie actor Ben Affleck.

Combs and Jennifer, however, did not have an easy romance. They had a lot of attention focused on them. Eventually, they each went their own way.

Jennifer again thought she found the love of her life, and on September 29, 2001, she married choreographer Cris Judd in a private ceremony in Calabasas, California. But this marriage didn't last any longer than her first and the couple was soon separated. In November 2002, Jennifer announced plans to marry movie actor Ben Affleck.

Jennifer Sings

*T*hough her love life has seemed a bit unstable, Jennifer's first love has always been dancing. She has also always loved to sing. After the success of films like *Selena*, Jennifer was approached by record executive Jeff Ayeroff about recording a CD. Sean "Puffy" Combs, her friend at the time, also encouraged the record company to hire Jennifer. Even the head of the company, Tommy Mottola, was brought in. In the end, she signed a contract with Sony Records to record her first album, *On the 6*.

The record was named after the number of the subway train in New York that Jennifer would take from the Bronx, her home, to get to the center of the city, Manhattan, where her father worked. Her drive to have a film and record career are simple, she said: "I've got to do it. I just thank God I have the opportunity."

Before her album was released, Jennifer received another lucky break—Latino singer Ricky Martin per-

Although Jennifer loves to sing and act, her first love has always been dancing.

Jennifer shooting a scene from her 2002 video All I Have

formed on the Grammy Awards show. According to *Billboard* writer John Lannert, many Latin singers owe some gratitude to Martin, whose February 24, 1999 performance on the Grammys sparked a wave of excitement nationwide for Latin music.

Although there are some Spanish-language songs on the record, including a duet with Marc Anthony, "*No Me Ames*/You Don't Love Me," Jennifer has scored her biggest hits on the album with English-language dance songs like "Waiting for Tonight," and rhythm-and-blues songs like "If You Had My Love." She had the help of several important music industry professionals like Emilio Estefan, record producer and husband of Gloria Estefan; Rick Wake, who has worked on records for Celine Dion; and even Sean Combs.

Jennifer presented an award and received her first Grammy nomination at The 42nd Annual Grammy Award Show.

One year after Ricky Martin's famous performance, *The 42nd Annual Grammy Award Show* featured several Latinos nominated in the Latin music categories but also in mainstream categories like Best Song and Best Album. Latino Carlos Santana took home top honors that night for his album *Supernatural*, but Jennifer also earned some attention. Besides the sexy dress she wore, Jennifer was an award presenter at the event and she received her first Grammy nomination for Best Dance

Recording for her song "Waiting for Tonight." She had already received four nominations for MTV Video Music Awards for her single "If You Had My Love."

On the 6 was a success from the time it was released, selling over two million copies worldwide. The first single, "If You Had My Love," stayed at the number-one spot in record sales for five weeks. She followed the success of *On the 6* with *J. Lo* (2001) and *This is Me...Then* (2002).

> *Whether she continues with her career depends on how hard Jennifer wants to continue to work.*

Whether she continues with both her singing and acting career does not depend on how well either does, because they've both been extremely successful, but on Jennifer, and how hard she wants to continue to work. "Of all the actors and actresses who have tried to become recording artists it's hard to think of one who has done quite as well," said Geoff Mayfield, director of *Billboard*, which tracks all record sales in the recording industry.

What the Future Holds

*A*t only 33 years old (in 2003) and at the top of her form, Jennifer has a story very similar to that of many young stars. She has always known that she wanted to be a star, and she made choices, like taking dancing lessons and opting out of a college education to seek fame and fortune as an entertainer. As she continues to grow as a star, her instincts about how to market herself remain strong.

Jennifer had a part in *The Cell*, which was released in 2000. In 2001, she starred in *The Wedding Planner* and *Angel Eyes*, followed by *Enough* and *Maid in Manhattan* in 2002. Upcoming projects in 2003 include *Jersey Girl* and *Tough Love* (formerly *Gigli*). She is also set to star opposite Richard Gere in a remake of *Shall We Dance?* L'Oréal cosmetics has hired her as a spokesperson.

But whatever she does, Jennifer remains aware of the important role she plays as a successful Latina. When asked by *Premiere* magazine to compare her career to the story of Cinderella or Rocky Balboa (from the Sylvester Stallone movie *Rocky*) she said, "I guess, in a way, it's a mix of both. But I don't see it [success] so much as a fairy tale as it is the result of working hard and wanting something so badly. I don't take anything for granted. I don't sleep, and I always take on more."

At 33 years old, Jennifer and her music and acting careers show no sign of slowing down.

For director Gregory Nava, who cast her in two of his films, the importance of Jennifer's success will be felt by many future Latinos who want a career as an entertainer. "She's helping to change the industry's perception of Latinos in leading roles. Having a name like Lopez in the old days was a real disadvantage. . . . Jennifer's a great role model for our community — to say, you can achieve your dream if you have passion."

She explained her ambitious nature to a reporter for *Honey* magazine: "I remember being fourteen or fifteen, and wanting so bad to be a better dancer and wanting to learn more, more, more. I remember telling my teacher, 'I just want to be better!'" In an article in *Premiere* she described her ambition this way: "I remember sitting in a movie theater so many times and seeing a trailer, like for *Terminator 2* or something, and being like, 'One day, that's going to be me.' I had to do it, or I'd kill myself. It's that extreme."

Jennifer's ambition has made her the highest paid Latina actress in Hollywood.

Her ambition has produced results. She has become the highest paid Latina actor in Hollywood. With the success of her albums and her success in Hollywood, Jennifer will continue to excite her fans and bring pride to the Latino community.

1970   born July 24 in the Bronx, New York
1975   begins taking dance lessons
1988   graduates from high school and decides not to go to college.
        Instead she lands a job in a theatrical show, *Golden Musicals
        of Broadway*, and tours Europe
1991   joins the cast of the television show *In Living Color* as a Fly
        Girl, part of the show's dance troupe
1995   director Gregory Nava casts Jennifer in *Mi Familia.*
1996   Nava casts Jennifer in the lead role as Selena Quintanilla
        Perez in his next film, *Selena*
1997   marries her first husband, Ojani Noa
1998   divorces Noa
1999   records her first CD, *On the 6*
2000   creates a sensation at the Grammy Awards with her new
        boyfriend Sean "Puffy" Combs
2001   releases second album, *J. Lo;* marries choreographer Cris
        Judd
2002   divorces Judd, announces plans to marry actor Ben Affleck

FILMOGRAPHY

1986	*My Little Girl*
1991	*In Living Color*
1993	*Nurses on the Line: The Crash of Flight 7* (TV Movie)
1995	*My Family/Mi Familia*
	Money Train
1996	*Jack*
	Blood and Wine
1997	*Selena*
	Anaconda
	U-Turn
1998	*Antz*
	Out of Sight
2000	*The Cell*
2001	*The Wedding Planner*
	Angel Eyes
2002	*Enough*
	Maid in Manhattan
2003	*Tough Love*
	Jersey Girl
	An Unfinished Life

DISCOGRAPHY

1999	*On the 6*
2001	*J. Lo*
2002	*J To Tha L-O! The Remixes*
	This is Me…Then

FOR FURTHER READING

Furman, Leah. *Jennifer Lopez*. Philadelphia: Chelsea House, 2001.

Marquez, Heron. *Latin Sensations*. Minneapolis, MN: Lerner Publications, 2001.

On the Web:

Official Web site
www.jenniferlopez.com

INDEX